The Heritage Collection

PHILLIS WHEATLEY

PIONEER AFRICAN AMERICAN POET

Letitia deGraft Okyere

Illustrated by Nazia Bibi

Lion's Historian PRESS
Amplifying Authentic Voices

Phillis Wheatley: Pioneer African American Poet

Copyright © 2021 by Letitia deGraft Okyere

Illustrator: Nazia Bibi

Interior design by: Nasim Malik Sarkar

Library of Congress Control Number: 2021920096

All rights reserved.

No part of this publication may be reproduced, stored in a retrieval system, a database and/or published in any form or by any means, electronic, mechanical, photocopying, recording or otherwise, without the prior written permission of the publisher.

ISBN 978-1-7374048-4-2 hardback
ISBN 978-1-7374048-5-9 ebook

Published by Lion's Historian Press
https://www.lionshistorian.net/

For

Louisa and Kelsey

CONTENTS

Captured 1

Journey on a Slave Ship to America 3

Sold as Chattel 5

Member of Wheatley Household 7

The Young Poet 9

New Found Fame 11

Confirmation by Leaders in Boston 13

A Trip to London 15

Freedom 17

Final Years 19

The Phillis Wheatley Legacy 21

Glossary 23
Quiz 24
References 25
Author's Note 26
Other Books in the Heritage Collection 27

Chapter 1

Captured

Little Sukai was out playing when she heard footsteps behind her. She turned to check and they looked like men from her village, so she continued playing. Suddenly, she felt strong arms grab her. Before she could scream for help, the men muffled her mouth with cloth and placed a sack over her. The kidnappers carried her away from her village, walking all day and night, only resting for short moments, unmoved by Sukai's tears.

After a few days, Sukai's kidnappers sold her to another slave trader. The slave trader took her through more forests until they arrived at a slave fort, in the Senegambia region, off the coast of Guinea, in West Africa. Here again, Sukai was sold to the slave traders at the fort. They put Sukai in a tiny dark dungeon with other captured men and women, none of them able to offer any comfort. Sukai spent many hours crying, knowing she would never see her family again.

Soon, the slave ship owned by a man called Timothy Finch docked at the port and the slave traders sold Sukai off to the ship's captain. Sukai would leave the land of her birth to a place unknown to her, like all the other captured slaves with her.

Chapter 2

Journey on a Slave Ship to America

When Sukai boarded the ship, the crew sent her below the deck to join the other slaves. They stripped Sukai almost naked, tied her up in chains, and put a brand on her back with a hot iron. Sukai screamed for mercy in her Wolof language, but no one came to help.

Sukai was placed between two women in the slave deck and could barely move as slaves were tightly packed. There was a lot of crying and shouting; some were injured from trying to break free from binding chains and others just worried about making the journey. The crew fed the slaves with just enough food to keep them alive. Sometimes, the men gave up their food for the women and handful of children. Sukai saw many slaves die, as the deck was dirty and barely any air made it through. She saw crew come down to take sick slaves away at night and the sick never returned.

The ship finally made it to America, arriving in Boston, Massachusetts, on July 11, 1761, after 245 days. Only 75 of the 96 slaves survived the journey to the North American coast, including little Sukai.

The records do not tell us her birth name, only that which her North American owners gave. However, she may have been called Sukai, a common Senegambian name, meaning *sky*. The name captures the hopes of a mother and father for their little daughter, sadly taken away when she was about seven or eight years old.

Chapter 3

Sold as Chattel

When the ship arrived in Boston, the workers on the ship made the slaves wash and after, rub themselves in palm oil to make them look stronger than they were. Many residents in Boston came to the ship in search of slaves. The captain quickly sold all the slaves on board his ship; however, no none seemed to want Sukai. There she stood at the market, very small and looking sickly, wrapped in nothing but a dirty old carpet. The captain thought he might not make any money from her.

The captain saw a woman ride up in her chaise carriage staring at the little girl and wondered if he might make a sale after all. The woman was Mrs. Susanna Wheatley, the wife of John Wheatley, a wealthy Boston merchant. Mrs. Wheatley asked to purchase Sukai and the relieved captain sold her for a mere ten pounds.

That day, Sukai joined Mrs. Wheatley in her carriage and went to the Wheatley family home in downtown Boston. The Wheatley family named the little slave girl Phillis and as was common practice, added the family's last name. The name *Phillis* was taken from the ship that took her away from her homeland to Boston.

Chapter 4

Member of Wheatley Household

Phillis became a member of the Wheatley household, which had two adult children, Nathaniel and Mary. For some reason, Mrs. Wheatley kept Phillis away from the other slaves working in her home. Soon, Phillis showed signs of a willingness to learn when she was seen trying to write.

Mary decided to teach Phillis to read and write, with approval from Mrs. Wheatley and the rest of the family. Mary taught Phillis English, Bible, and Latin. Within sixteen months of her arrival at the Wheatley home, Phillis learned how to speak English and could read difficult parts of the Bible. Mary introduced writings by the poets Alexander Pope and John Milton.

Chapter 5

The Young Poet

Phillis improved in her studies in leaps and bounds. Some four years later, she wrote her first poem. Two years after, in 1767, Mrs. Wheatley submitted one of Phillis' poems to a local newspaper and it was published.

In 1770, on King's Street in Boston, close to the Wheatley home, the Boston Massacre occurred. It was a riot between American colonists — who wanted freedom from the British — and British soldiers. Phillis wrote a poem honoring some of those who died or suffered injuries on King Street. Phillis wrote other poems commenting on issues of the times.

The Wheatley's were proud of Phillis' natural gift and they would invite friends to their home to talk with Phillis. Phillis discussed her poems and views on literature. Many of the guests left the Wheatley home impressed by the skill of the slave girl.

Chapter 6

New Found Fame

Phillis converted to Christianity through Mrs. Wheatley's influence. This exposed Phillis to Bible teachings of the evangelical movement within the Anglican Church, known as Methodism. When Reverend George Whitefield, a founder of Methodism, died in 1770 when visiting Boston, Phillis decided to write a poem in his memory.

In writing the Whitefield poem, Phillis wisely referred to Selina Hastings, the wealthy Countess of Huntingdon in Britain who was close friends with Whitefield. Phillis then sent a copy of the poem with a letter, expressing her sympathy at Whitefield's death, to the Countess of Huntingdon.

Phillis' poem was widely published in Boston and other North American cities like New York and Philadelphia. When the Countess of Huntingdon received Phillis' letter, the poem was also published in London the next year. Phillis now enjoyed international fame.

Chapter 7

Confirmation by Leaders in Boston

Phillis continued to build up a collection of poems. As Phillis' volume of work increased with publications of single poems, the Wheatley family decided to have a selection published. Several advertisements were placed in a local paper in 1772, for contributions to cover publication costs, listing 28 poems by Phillis.

Unfortunately, Mrs. Wheatley was unable to collect enough contributions. At the time, people did not believe that an African could be so creative and therefore, it was impossible for an African slave to produce poems. Phillis and the family believed that if others confirmed Phillis' ability, she would get the contributions she needed for the publication of a complete set of poems.

At a meeting in Boston in 1772, Phillis obtained the needed written confirmation by 18 important men of society. The group of men included the Governor of Massachusetts, as well as authors and church leaders. These men signed their names to a document confirming to the world that Phillis was indeed the author of the poems noted.

Chapter 8
A Trip to London

Sadly, the declaration made no difference in Boston. Phillis was disappointed, but Mrs. Wheatley suggested they ask the Countess of Huntingdon for help. It was easier for African authors to be published in England. The English publisher called Archibald Bell agreed to publish the collection of poems. The Countess of Huntingdon allowed Phillis to dedicate the book to her but asked that a picture of Phillis be printed on the book cover.

During this time, as Phillis wasn't feeling well, the Wheatley family recommended she travel to London with Nathaniel in May 1773 for some fresh sea air which might help. Phillis visited significant London sites like the Tower of London and met with several leaders, including Granville Sharp, who campaigned to abolish slavery. Her meeting with King George was canceled because she had to return to America to help a sick Mrs. Wheatley.

After Phillis departed from London, her book was published. *Poems on Various Subjects Religious and Moral* contained almost forty poems. The book was well-received in both England and North America with reviews by well-known authors and historians.

Chapter 9

Freedom

During her trip to London, which occurred after the British Somerset legal case of 1772, Phillis bargained for her freedom with Nathaniel. The Somerset case stated that slaves were not property but persons with certain legal rights. In addition, Phillis sent a copy of the documentation that provided her freedom and protected her property to an associate in the U.K., in the event, the Wheatley family changed their mind after she returned to Boston.

Phillis was freed by the Wheatley family when she returned to America with Nathaniel. However, she stayed with the Wheatley family and continued to add new poems to her collection even after Susanna Wheatley died in 1774. Phillis looked for an opportunity to publish a second volume.

Phillis also began to express her desire for equality. Her letter to Reverend Samson Occom, a missionary to the Native Americans in 1774, discussed the need for freedom and liberty. Occom regularly communicated with Phillis on matters of public interest. Reverend Samuel Hopkins, an abolitionist of slavery, sought Phillis' help as a partner in spreading Christianity in Africa. Through Hopkins, Phillis was introduced to Philip Quaque, the African missionary to the Gold Coast, now Ghana. Quaque and Wheatley became the first authors of African descent to have their writings published together.

Chapter 10

Final Years

Phillis Wheatley continued to seek help with publishing a second book. Unfortunately, the American Revolution broke out in 1765 and readers forgot about her work. To drum up interest in her again, Phillis composed a poem in honor of General George Washington in October 1775 and sent him a copy with a letter. Washington got the poem published in Virginia in 1776 and invited Phillis for a visit, which she accepted.

In 1779, Phillis placed several advertisements in Boston newspapers, advertising poems and wanting to build up contributions with her intention to dedicate her second book to Benjamin Franklin, one of the founding fathers of the United States of America. Yet still, she had no success. Phillis continued trying to get her poems published and placed an advert in a Boston paper in September 1784.

Phillis sadly died a few months later, in December of 1784, unable to publish her second book of poems. She was about thirty years old at death.

Epilogue
The Phillis Wheatley Legacy

Phillis Wheatley was the first African American and the second woman in America to publish poems. Wheatley's poems acquired international fame and received praise from well-known authors. Even though her second book got lost, copies of some of her poems have been discovered.

In honor of her contribution to the literary arts, there are many buildings, including schools and libraries, named after Phillis Wheatley. The Boston Women's Memorial, dedicated in 2003 to three women who had an impact on the city's development, includes a statue of Phillis Wheatley.

The poetess has been criticized for not writing much about her experiences as a slave, yet she condemned the horrors of slavery in poems and letters with those she associated with. Phillis' achievements were important for ending slavery because she showed the creative ability of black people. She set the pace for the growth of African American poetry.

Phillis Wheatley may have had a short life and the last years of her life spent in financial hardship, but she succeeded as a poet when many thought Africans were not intelligent people. Phillis' life story is an inspirational one. She was a pioneering poet who rose above the brutality of racial inequality, producing at least 145 poems. Wheatley remains of interest to modern reviewers. In 2005, a recently discovered letter written by Wheatley in 1776 sold for $250,000 at an auction.

Glossary

Senegambia	A region in West Africa that included Senegal and The Gambia.
Brand(ing)	The process when a mark is burned into the skin of a slave using a hot iron, for identification purposes.
Wolof	A language spoken by people from Senegal, The Gambia and Mauritania, in West Africa.
Boston Massacre	A riot between American colonists — who wanted freedom from the British — and British soldiers.
Countess	The wife or widow of a count or earl; a title of noble persons in Europe.
Methodism	A Christian group started by a man called John Wesley.
Anglican Church	A Christian group, also known as the Church of England.
Granville Sharp	A British man who campaigned for the ending of slavery.
Somerset Legal Case	This case in England decided that slaves were not property but persons with certain legal rights.
Slavery Abolitionist	A person who seeks to end slavery.

Quiz

1. Where was Phillis Wheatley born?

    (a) America

    (b) London

    (c) Boston

    (d) West Africa

2. What was the name of the slave ship she travelled on?

    (a) The Branch

    (b) The Phillis

    (c) The Clotilda

    (d) The Brooks

3. How much was Phillis sold for at the slave market?

    (a) 20 pounds

    (b) 50 pounds

    (c) 10 pounds

    (d) 100 pounds

4. Who did Phillis dedicate her first book to?

    (a) The Countess of Huntingdon

    (b) The Duke of Richmond

    (c) The Earl of Grafton

    (d) The Countess of Bedford

Quiz answers: DBCA

References

Carretta, Vincent. *Phillis Wheatley: Biography of a Genuis in Bondages*. Athens, University of Georgia Press, 2011.

Brooks, Joanna. "Our Phillis, Ourselves." *American Literature*, vol. 82, no. 1, 2010, pp. 1-28.

Gates, Henry Louis Jr. *The Trials of Phillis Wheatley: America's First Black Poet and Her Encounters with the Founding Fathers*. New York, Basic Civitas Books, 2003.

Applegate, Ann. "Phillis Wheatley: Her Critics and her Contribution." *Negro American Literature Forum*, vol. 9, no. 4, 1975, pp.123-126.

Author's Note

Through the Heritage Collection's historical biographies for children, the author endeavors to tell the stories of men and women of African descent who changed the course of events within their circles of influence.

Historical biographies are important for child development. When a child can see him- or herself represented in the life of people who grew up to effect social, economic, or political change, he or she is more likely to be inspired to meet and overcome life's challenges.

Thus, the author's purpose is simple: to enable children to fulfill their destinies by seeing themselves through others who rose above difficulties to bring about change.

Other Books in the Heritage Collection

The story of Queen Amina is an important one for girls everywhere. Explore how Queen Amina gained a reputation as a fearless warrior, breaking barriers at a time when men dominated most aspects of life. Queen Amina's life will inspire and encourage you to be fearless.

Who was Queen Nandi? She is referred to as one of the greatest mothers that ever lived. As a queen mother, she saw her son Shaka become one of the greatest kings of the Zulu people and builder of the Zulu empire. Read her story and learn how she made her mark in history.

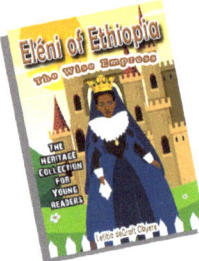
Eléni was a princess from Hadiya who became the wife of Emperor Zara Yaqob in 1445. Eléni guided the reign of five emperors and fearlessly challenged the leading role men played in society as an empress, queen mother and regent. Eléni's story will inspire girls and women everywhere to rise above difficult circumstances and fulfill their destiny.

R.J. Ghartey saw no limits to what he could achieve. As a young man, he rejected traditional paths of fishing and farming and learned a different trade. Through this, he became an influential business entrepreneur. In addition, Ghartey played an important role in local politics and found ways to improve the lives of those in his community. In telling Ghartey's story, the author hopes to encourage children with different dreams to pursue their destinies past challenges that they may face.

www.ingramcontent.com/pod-product-compliance
Lightning Source LLC
Chambersburg PA
CBHW041704160426
43209CB00017B/1744